ART AND CRAFT SKILLS

PAINTING

Donna McQueen

SEA-TO-SEA

Mankato Collingwood London

This edition first published in 2006 by
Sea-to-Sea Publications
1980 Lookout Drive
North Mankato
Minnesota 56003

Printed in China

Library of Congress Cataloging-in-Publication Data

McQueen, Donna.
   Painting/ by Donna McQueen.
      p. cm.. – (Art and craft skills)
   Includes index.
   ISBN 1-932889-84-1
   1. Painting–Technique–Juvenile literature. I. Title. II. Art and craft skills (North Mankato, Minn.)

ND1146.M36 2005
751–dc22

                                                       2004063702

9 8 7 6 5 4 3 2

Published by arrangement with the Watts Publishing Group Ltd., London

Series editor: Kyla Barber
Designer: Lisa Nutt
Illustrator: Lynda Murray
Photographer: Steve Shott
Art director: Robert Walster

Contents

Getting Started

Painting is a way of making marks with liquid color. The marks are made by moving the liquid around on a surface. Look carefully at what you want to paint. Think about colors, shapes, and textures. You can also create moods and feelings with paint.

Basic Methods

1. Color Mixing: There are thousands of colors in the world around us and they can all be created by mixing just a few.

2. Brushes: Hold your brush like a pencil, on the fattest part of the wood. Use it like a spoon to lift powder paint. Use different brushes to make different marks.

3. Experiments: Brushes are not the only tools you can use for painting. Marks can be made with almost anything—fingers, oaktag, feathers, rags, sponges, plastic forks, or cotton spools. Paint can be wet, dry, smooth, rough, thick, splattered, or dripped.

Looking is very important when you paint. Careful looking helps you to understand the shape, texture, color, and form of different objects.

This is the best way to set things out if you are right–handed. If you're left–handed, you might prefer the paints on your left. The dark colors should be at the front of the palette so you don't spill them in the light colors when you carry a brushful onto your mixing plate.

Primary Colors

The three primary colors are red, blue, and yellow. They cannot be made by mixing with other colors. But with the three primary colors and white you can make any color. You can also make your own black paint using blue, red, and yellow. You will need mostly blue as it is the darkest of the three colors.

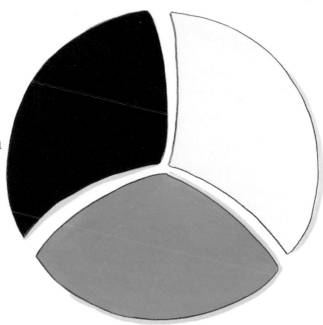

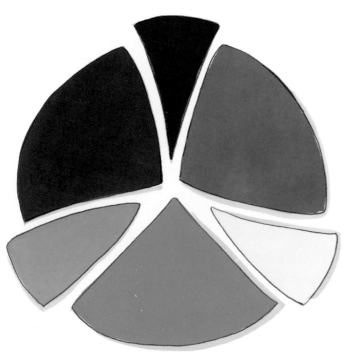

Secondary Colors

The secondary colors are made by mixing two primary colors together. Red and yellow make orange, yellow and blue make green, blue and red make purple. Brown can be made by mixing all three secondary colors. Every color can be made lighter by adding white.

Painting Supplies

There are many different kinds of paints, brushes, and paper. But you don't need many supplies to get started. Check the store key to find out where to buy them.

Store key

Art supply store

Craft store

Drugstore

Stationery store

Supermarket

Toy store

Paints

1. Liquid Paint comes in large squeeze bottles. It is simple to use and can be easily mixed. You can make the paint thinner with water, but you can only thicken it by adding powder paint or white glue ( ).

2. Powder Paint can be mixed easily with other colors and with a little water. Add more powder to make the paint thicker. You can also use powder paint without any water (see pages 16–17) ( ).

3. Acrylic paints come in tubes and can be used for painting on objects ( ).

4. Watercolors come in cakes. They produce very bright colors or extremely pale, delicate colors, depending on how much water you add. They are very good for painting on wet paper and for tiny details ( ).

5. Block Paints are solid cubes of water-based paint. You can mix them with a little water on the surface of the cube itself. There is very little waste with these paints ( ).

6. Fabric Paints There are many kinds of fabric paint. Some are permanent dyes, others will wash out. Fabric paints come in liquid and powder form ( ).

Other materials

7. Wide–based water container that is not easy to knock over, but an old mug or jam jar will do ( ).

8. Tray palette or large plate, for mixing paint ( ).

9. A variety of brushes. Different–shaped bristles give different effects ( ).

10. Other tools for applying paint: old plastic fork, large comb, oaktag, rags, craft sticks, sponges, rollers, straws, or medicine droppers ( ).

11. Oaktag and a variety of paper: textured paper, smooth paper, and paper of different colors ( ).

12. Chalk— white or yellow, to draw a design ( ).

13. White glue ( ).

14. Mixing equipment, e.g., plastic spoons, old pitcher, large bowl, or old margarine tubs ( ).

15. Two pairs of scissors—one for paper and one for fabric ( ).

16. Polycotton cloth or old sheet.

17. Cardboard box and tape to hold fabric while painting ( ).

18. Materials for adding texture, e.g., rice, grass cuttings, sand, or seeds.

Keep it Tidy

19. Sponges for wiping brushes, cleaning up messes, and for painting.

20. Old shirt with sleeves rolled up.

21. Newspaper or plastic sheet to protect work surfaces.

Looking for ideas?

Try to find prints of work by famous artists such as Claude Monet, L.S. Lowry, J.M.W. Turner, and others. Check the glossary to find out more about some of the artists mentioned in this book.

Color Mixing

Mix powder paints together to create new colors. By adding just tiny amounts of color at a time, you can make hundreds of different shades.

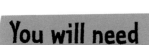

- ★ powder paints
- ★ water
- ★ chalk
- ★ scissors
- ★ small paintbrush
- ★ palette
- ★ smooth paper
- ★ mixing plate
- ★ oaktag

1. Use your chalk (white for colored paper, yellow for white paper) to draw a crescent moon. Chalk is better than pencil for drawing—it won't show through your paint.

2. Start with the lighter colors and work up to the darker ones. Use the brush like a spoon to lift some yellow paint and tap the paint gently off onto a small area of the plate.

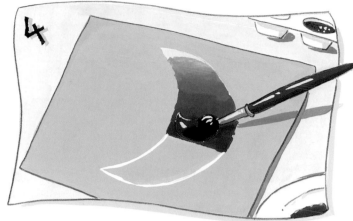

3. Dip the tip of your brush into the water. Mix a drop of water into the yellow paint. It should be thick and creamy. If it's lumpy, take another tiny drop of water. If it's thin, take a little more paint. Paint one tip of your moon pure yellow.

4. Without washing your brush, dip it into the red. Mix it into the yellow paint on your plate. Paint the next section of the moon. For each new section, add a little more of the red powder. You don't need to wash your brush.

5. You can make planets with rings—like Saturn—using your color–mixing skills. Cut out a circle and an oval from oaktag. The oval needs to be wider than the circle. Paint both shapes. Cut a slit in the oval and slide in the circle.

Now Try These

Christmas Tree
Cut out two Christmas trees from oaktag. Use your color–mixing technique to paint them. Cut a slit in the top of each one, down to about halfway. Slot them together.

Snake in the Grass
Cut out and paint a snake. Start with a light color at one end and add more and more of a darker color as you go along.

Decorating

Now that you have colored some shapes, you can start to decorate them. Try this colorful rooster.

You will need

- scissors
- damp sponge
- mixing tray
- powder paints
- paper
- chalk
- small paintbrush

1. Draw the outline of the body and head of a rooster with chalk. Cut out the main shape of the rooster, then draw some feathers, two legs, an eye, and a crest. Cut these out too.

2. The body starts with a pure yellow beak. Add red powder a little at a time. Paint the feathers using different colors—add white to green, white to blue, and yellow to red again.

3. For the crest you can use the same method of color mixing, but instead of blending the colors together, you can paint stripes. Make each stripe slightly darker than the last.

4. To decorate, use a light–colored paint on a dark background and a dark color on a light background. Paint stripes, dots, crosses, zigzags, or circles. Keep them neat.

5. Try adding a little blue to the yellow. Then add white to all your colors for lighter shades. Paint tiny patterns among the other patterns. With the last color, paint the eye.

Now Try These

Decorated Box
Use different colors, shades, and patterns to decorate a box. Try not to follow the edges of the box in your design.

Eggs
You can paint and decorate other 3–D objects in just the same way. Try these eggs.

Egg Cups
Paint a pattern on an egg cup or mug. If you want a washable product, check the paint manufacturer's instructions.

PAINTER'S TIPS

◆ Make sure your background paint is dry before you start to decorate.
◆ Never leave your brushes in water—they will curl at the end and be damaged.

Backgrounds

Backgrounds need never be boring to look at or to paint. Often it is a useful rule to paint everything in the order it existed. Which existed first, the sky or a house? The sky—so paint that first.

You will need

- scissors
- pencil
- paper
- paintbrush
- cloth or rags
- damp sponge
- oaktag pieces
- powder paints

1. To quickly fill in a large area, such as sky or land, try using a sponge to apply a textured layer of paint. Remember—sky and land have many different colors in them—not just one.

2. Try making dappled patterns with a piece of cloth. This is useful for forests and clouds where the light is patchy. Famous Impressionist painters such as Claude Monet and Georges Seurat used dappled effects.

Castle

On a piece of black paper draw the outline of a castle in pencil. Cut around your pencil line with a pair of scissors to create a silhouette and stick this onto your background.

Now Try These

Making Waves

Make up some thick and creamy blue paint using blue and white powder paints. Don't mix the two colors completely. Use a stiff piece of oaktag to scoop up the paint and pull it along the paper to spread the paint and shape it into waves.

Sunset in Africa

Paint a sunset background using a cloth or rag to apply the paint. The clouds are added to the painted background. You can stick on silhouettes of African animals.

Drip, Pour, Splatter

You can drip, pour, blow, or splatter paint onto paper. The American artist Jackson Pollock is famous for this type of painting. Protect the area all around your work and experiment with these methods.

You will need

- ★ big paintbrush
- ★ old pitcher
- ★ medicine dropper
- ★ squeezy liquid paints
- ★ thick paper
- ★ straws
- ★ scissors
- ★ paper
- ★ pencil

1. First, try dripping the paint from a medicine dropper. Drip different colors and different–sized drops.

2. Mix the color you want in a pitcher. Try pouring a thin, steady stream of paint onto the paper by tilting the pitcher slightly.

3. Put a blob of very thin wet paint on the paper and blow hard on it to send it in all directions. Try using a straw to blow through.

4. Dip a large paintbrush in paint. Don't touch the paper with it—just flick it downward, quite hard, to splatter paint onto the paper.

14

Now Try These

Covered Books
Draw a simple design on paper. Snip out the center shape with a small pair of scissors to make a stencil. Stick the paper stencil onto a plain book cover. Drip, pour, blow, or splatter the paint through the stencil opening.

Musical Covers
Brighten up your CD or tape cases with brightly colored patterns.

Volcano!
Splatter techniques are great for making explosions or fireworks. They are also good for mood pictures (see pages 26–27).

Dry Painting

Here is a simple way of painting without using any water. You can create wonderful patterns with dry powder paint.

You will need
♦ oaktag ♦ powder paints ♦ paper ♦ plate ♦ scissors ♦ brush ♦ spoon ♦ straws

1. To mix new shades, spoon a little of two colors onto your plate and gently stir them together with the dry brush. Dip the tip of the dry brush into your new color.

2. When you want to change color don't wash your brush—just tap the handle on the side of the plate to knock the powder off. Then dip it into your next color.

Create a beautiful sunset. On dark paper make a yellow circle for the sun. Then use your fingers to create a swirling, glowing sky.

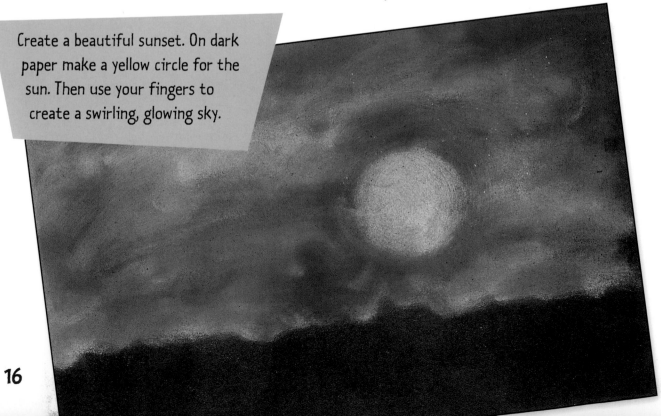

The artist J.M.W. Turner painted swirling studies of light and movement. Also look at work by L.S. Lowry who is famous for his paintings of skies and smoky chimneys.

Chimney

Dry powder paints are very good for skies, clouds, and smoke. Here a cutout skyline stencil was stuck on to blue paper, and the sky was painted with dry powder.

Now Try These

Flowers

Draw and cut out flower shapes from colored oaktag. Use powder paints to shade in the shapes. Take a straw to make the stalk of the flower—the bendy kind are best. Ask an adult to make a small—less than $1/2$ inch (1 centimeter)—slit across the top of the straw using a craft knife. Slide the flower in.

Wet Painting

We've seen how you can paint without water—now try using lots! For this kind of painting try different kinds of paints for different effects—watercolors, powder, liquid, or block. You also need very smooth paper. Construction paper does not work well because it quickly soaks up the water.

1. Using a large, clean brush, paint a layer of clean water over the area you want to paint.

2. Now, using different kinds of paints see what happens when you drop or paint color onto the wet area. If the paper dries, use a clean brush to wet it again.

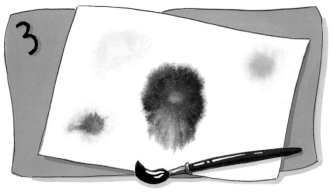

3. Which paints work best? Try mixing them thickly, then thinly using more water. Use this method to paint water, sky, landscapes, or pictures that create a mood (see pages 26–27).

Lily Pond

Make a wet painting of a pond. Paint lily pads and flowers separately, and stick them onto your background. Look at Monet's famous lily pond paintings.

PAINTER'S TIP

◎ When the paper is dry you can decorate it even more with a fine felt pen or paintbrush.

Now Try These

Jam Jar Lantern

Take a jam jar and cut a rectangle of paper that will just wrap around it. Wet paint the paper and let it dry. With sharp scissors cut lines into the paper, parallel to the shorter sides. The cuts should stop about 1 inch (2.5 centimeters) in from the long edges. Tape the paper around your jar and place a small night–light inside.

Wrap up presents using your own wet-painted paper

Stationery

You can cut out shapes to use as gift tags or to cover books. You can also make cards and matching envelopes.

Painting on Fabric

There are many different kinds of fabric paints available. Read the manufacturer's instructions carefully before you start and choose the kind best suited to your project. Normal liquid or powder paints can also be used if you don't need a washable product.

You will need

★ fabric paints and other paints
★ polycotton cloth or an old sheet
★ cardboard box and tape
★ brushes   ★ fabric scissors
★ water   ★ chalk
★ craft stick
★ mixing tray

1. Sketch a design on paper. Cut a piece of cloth or old sheet to the size you want. Stretch it by taping it smoothly over an open box. Mark out the design on your cloth in chalk. This dragon was painted with ordinary liquid paints.

2. Now try using some damp cloth. Set it up in the same way. Put a drop of runny paint on your wet fabric and watch it spread. Gradually, new colors will come out. Try adding other drops to run softly in.

Now Try These

Cushion Cover
This was decorated with powder paint. You need only a very tiny amount—use a craft stick to lift a tiny pile of powder onto your palette and mix it with plenty of water.

Silk Scarf
To paint on a piece of silk, select a special silk paint, and read the instructions carefully.

Many fabric paints wash out. Check the instructions.

Starting Points

This technique is all about building up from a small piece of an existing pattern or texture. Your finished picture might end up looking very different from the original.

You will need

- old magazines
- candy wrappers
- wrapping paper
- scissors • glue
- white paper • paints • small brush
- water
- mixing plate

1. Cut out small squares from candy wrappers. Choose a piece that has interesting shapes and colors in it. Glue it in the middle of a sheet of paper. Now you have a starting point.

2. Using a small brush see if you can begin to extend the pattern by copying the marks on it. Use your color–mixing skills first to match the colors on the wrapper as closely as you can.

3 Try to continue the shapes and colors out from the wrapper onto your paper. Don't worry about what the picture was like originally. Look only at the colors, shapes, and textures— and let your imagination go.

Now Try These

Picture Strip
Use a strip cut from a picture in a magazine. Or you could use a photograph —perhaps one of yourself!

Fake Frames
Take some real textures as your starting points— wood, brick, stone— whatever you can find that has a variety of colors and shapes within it.

PAINTER'S TIPS

◆ Find work by famous artists. Copy their style, color, and technique—this will help you to develop new painting skills.

Hidden Details

Paint a picture packed with detail—then hide some areas under flaps. Match up the flaps with the rest of the picture.

You will need

- watercolors or block paints
- small brushes
- mixing tray
- water
- magazines or books to use as reference for your subjects
- glue
- scissors

1. Use a medium–sized sheet of paper, watercolors or block paints, and small brushes. Paint the background first. This one is going to be an underwater scene.

2. Add a few details to your background—seaweed and coral. Take a look at some photos first. What color is seaweed—light apple green or a darker forest green?

3. Using your tiny brush, paint some creatures in the sea. Look at photos of fish in books to help you get them right.

4. On a new sheet of paper, paint separate clumps of seaweed or rocks. These will be used to hide the creatures.

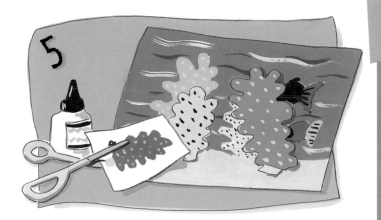

5. Cut them out carefully when they are dry, but remember to leave a little tab. Stick the tabs onto the painting to hide the creature under the flap.

Now try these

Jungle Fever
The jungle is full of hidden creatures. Tigers, snakes, and insects lurk behind the leaves.

Nasty Surprise
Make a hidden scene inside a folded burger card. Paint the outside to look like a bun, and put a burger, some lettuce, or even a worm inside!

Moods and Feelings

Painting is a very good way of showing your feelings. Artists are able to put their moods and feelings into their work. When we look at a picture, we can share the emotions the artist felt when the picture was painted.

You will need

- paints—a variety of kinds
- brushes
- water
- paper

1. Start with a picture of something familiar. Use watery paints and soft flowing brush strokes. This creates a calm, happy mood picture.

2. A mood painting does not need to be a picture of anything real. Shapes or colors might help you to express your feelings.

Calm, peaceful feelings often make you think of warm colors and rounded shapes.

3. Angry or sad feelings often make us think of dark, dull colors—blues, purples, blacks, and grays. Sharp edges make us feel uneasy.

4. A happy picture can be made with bright splashes of color and soft shapes.

What brushes and other tools would you choose for different moods? Think about how you move the brush to match the different feelings.

PAINTER'S TIPS

◆ Listen to a piece of music, perhaps one you have never heard before. Paint along to it, listening for the different moods and choosing colors and shapes to go with them.

Now Try This

Swirling, flowing, flicking, dabbing, and splattering (some of the methods we used on pages 14–15) are also good for mood pictures.

Fingers and Forks

You don't have to paint with a brush—try using your fingers, forks, combs, and sticks to move the paint around.

You will need

- ★ powder paints
- ★ old fork, comb, stick
- ★ white glue
- ★ large plastic tray
- ★ thick paper
- ★ clear plastic sheet or plastic "loose-leaf" folder, cut in two

1. Take a clear plastic sheet or a plastic "loose-leaf" folder. Mix four different shades of red and orange. Make the paint very thick by adding white glue. Put a large blob of each color on the plastic.

2. Use your fingers to spread the paint all over the plastic, almost to the edges, but don't mix all the paint together— keep some of each color and some of the new colors where they mix.

3. Scrape lines in the paint using a stick or old fork, so that areas of the plastic show through. Try to create a "fiery" effect. Stop when you are happy with your design.

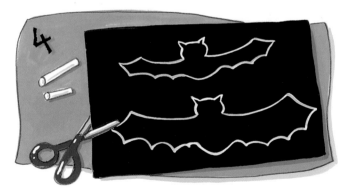

4. Take a piece of black paper. Draw and cut out two bat shapes. They can be different sizes. Stick them onto the fiery background and hang your picture in a window.

Now Try These

Ship on a Stormy Sea

Create a stormy sea background using the same technique—use your fingers to make waves with thick blue and white paints. Cut out or paint a ship to sail on your stormy sea.

Pieces of Fruit

Try drawing objects with your fingers—you can use really thick paint to produce texture, depth, and interesting colors.

Mixing Media

You can create many different effects using paint on its own, but you can add even more variety by mixing other textures with it.

You will need

★ liquid paints ★ white glue ★ paper plate
★ rice, seeds, sand, grass cuttings, feathers
★ mixing tray or margarine tubs
★ thick paper or object to paint on
★ references from magazines or photographs

1. Liquid paints are easiest to mix with other things. Sketch your picture in chalk then mix the color you need. Carefully sprinkle in any materials you want to mix with the paint. You could try rice, sand, or seeds.

2. Using a large brush, stir your chosen material into the paint. It should still be liquid enough to paint with but feel fairly thick. A small amount of white glue mixed in helps to stop the paint flaking off when it dries.

3. Use the different textures you have mixed for different areas of your picture. Rice could be used for the house and roof, grass cuttings for meadows, and sand for fields of wheat. You can also mix white glue with paint by itself—it will dry shiny. Clean your brush after using it with white glue.

Now Try These

Masks

Make a mask from a paper plate, cut out holes for the eyes, and paint on a design. Stick on feathers, rice, string, and paper for added effect.

Decorated Plant Pot

You can use this technique to decorate 3–D objects too.

Glossary of Artists

IMPRESSIONISTS were a group of artists that moved away from a traditional way of painting—trying to draw the world as it actually was. They painted pictures that give a feeling, or "impression," of light or movement, rather than trying to produce a "photographic" type of work (pages 4, 18–19).

L. S. LOWRY painted the industrial mills and factories in the north of England. He used dull colors and showed matchstick people rushing through cold streets (pages 7, 17).

Claude MONET experimented with paint, color, and light. He is particularly famous for a series of paintings of lilies on a pond. He drew the same picture again and again, but at different times of day and throughout the year so that the light and air changed above the water. He was an "Impressionist" painter (pages 7, 12, 19).

Jackson POLLOCK dripped, poured, and splattered paint onto his canvas and used sticks and knives to swirl it into abstract shapes. These techniques became known as "Action Painting." He wanted to let his feelings flood into his work (page 14).

Georges SEURAT painted views of the river in Paris. He is well known for painting tiny dots of pure color to make up a picture (pages 12).

J. M. W. TURNER is famous for his swirling, glowing paintings of storms, high seas. and smoke rising through the air (pages 7, 17).

Index